WORLD'S GREATEST
CHRISTMAS MUSIC

55 of the Most Popular Holiday Songs and Solos

Celebrate the season with dozens of beloved Christmas songs from throughout the ages! Packed with traditional carols, festive standards, and holiday hits, this sheet music anthology promises a lifetime of music-making fun for all occasions, from family sing-alongs to Christmas concerts.

ISBN-13: 978-0-7390-6284-5

EXCLUSIVELY DISTRIBUTED BY

CONTENTS

ANGELS WE HAVE HEARD ON HIGH

TRADITIONAL

Chorus:

From THE POLAR EXPRESS

BELIEVE

Words and Music by
ALAN SILVESTRI and GLEN BALLARD

Moderately slow ♩ = 80

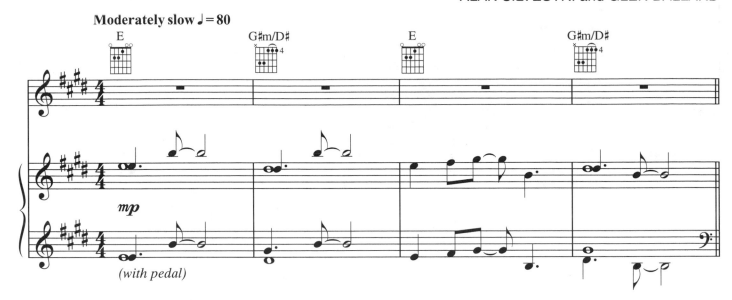

Verse:

1. Chil - dren___ sleep - ing,___ snow is soft - ly fall - ing.___
2. Trains move___ quick - ly___ to their jour - ney's end.

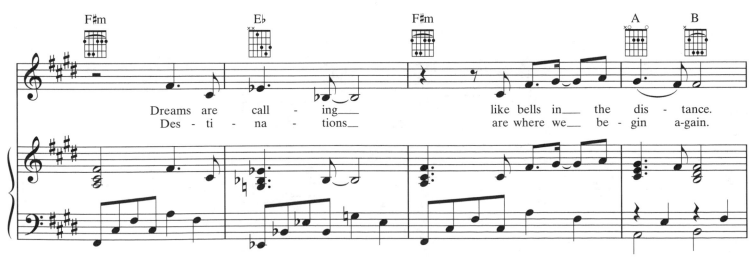

Dreams are call - ing___ like bells in___ the dis - tance.
Des - ti - na - tions___ are where we___ be - gin a - gain.

Believe - 4 - 1

ALL I WANT FOR CHRISTMAS IS YOU
(A Christmas Love Song)

Lyrics by
ALAN and MARILYN BERGMAN

Music by
JOHNNY MANDEL

CELEBRATE ME HOME

Lyrics by
KENNY LOGGINS

Music by
KENNY LOGGINS and BOB JAMES

THE CHRISTMAS BLUES

Words by
SAMMY CAHN

Music by
DAVID HOLT

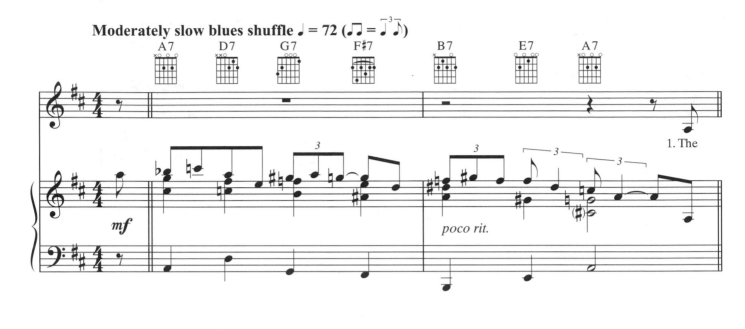

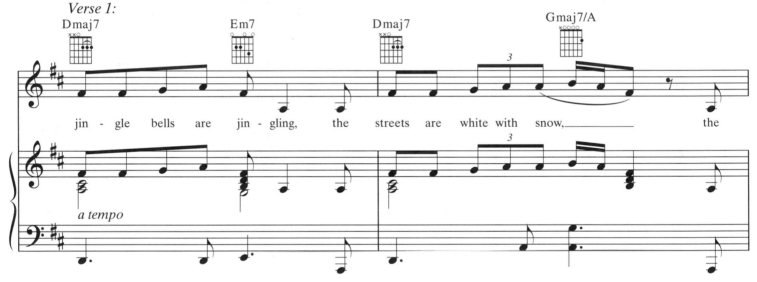

The Christmas Blues - 6 - 1

CHRISTMAS CANON

Words and Music by
PAUL O'NEILL

Christmas Canon - 5 - 1

CHRISTMAS EVE/SARAJEVO 12/24

Music by
PAUL O'NEILL and ROBERT KINKEL

Christmas Eve/Sarajevo 12/24 - 7 - 3

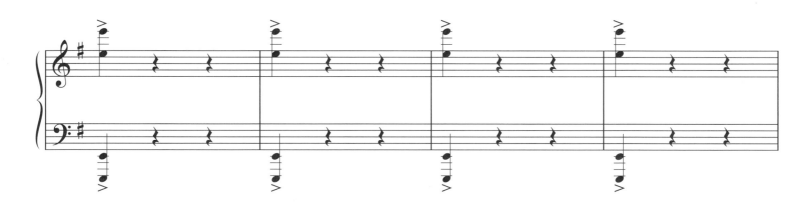

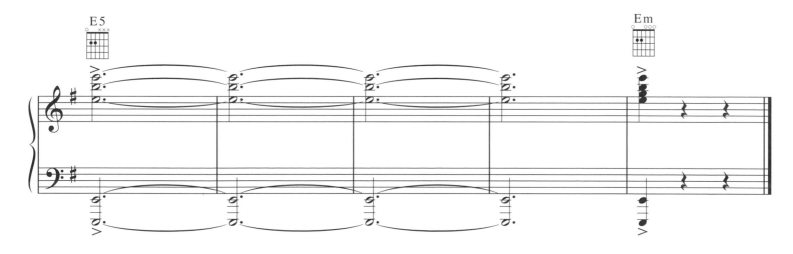

Christmas Eve/Sarajevo 12/24 - 7 - 7

THE CHRISTMAS SHOES

Words and Music by
LEONARD AHLSTROM and
EDDIE CARSWELL

Mom's been sick for quite__ a while.__ And I know these shoes would make__ her smile.__ And I

want her to look beau - ti - ful___ if Ma - ma__ meets Je - sus__ to -

night.

2. He count-ed

Verse 2:

pen - nies for__ what seemed__ like years.__ Then the cash-ier said, "Son, there's not e-nough here."__

hur - ry, Sir,___ Dad - dy says there's not much time.___ You see,

Mom's been sick for quite___ a while.___ And I know these shoes would make___ her smile.___ And I

To Coda ⊕

want her to look beau - ti - ful___ if Ma - ma___ meets Je - sus___ to -

Bridge:

night._____ I knew I caught a glimpse___ of heav - en's love___ as he

COMING HOME FOR CHRISTMAS

Words and Music by
JIM BRICKMAN, VICTORIA SHAW
and RICHIE McDONALD

Chorus:

1.
Am7 D7sus Gsus2 sus4 G
home for Christ - mas.
C F(9)
2.
Gsus2 sus4 G(9)
Christ - mas.
Bridge:
C2 G/B
Wan - na hear all a - bout all the things you're do - ing and
Am7 Em7 G C2 G/B
make up for lost time.
Tell you what I've been through, laugh like we al - ways do.

THE CHRISTMAS WALTZ

Words by
SAMMY CAHN

Music by
JULE STYNE

The Christmas Waltz - 3 - 1

DING DONG MERRILY ON HIGH

Traditional,
Arranged by DAVID DOWNES

Ding Dong Merrily on High - 7 - 3

Ding Dong Merrily on High - 7 - 5

58

DECK THE HALL

TRADITIONAL

DO THEY KNOW IT'S CHRISTMAS?

(Feed the World)

Medium Rock

Words and Music by
BOB GELDOF and MIDGE URE

THE FIRST NOEL

TRADITIONAL

68

The First Noel - 3 - 2

FELIZ NAVIDAD

Words and Music by
JOSÉ FELICIANO

FROSTY THE SNOWMAN

Words and Music by
STEVE NELSON and JACK ROLLINS

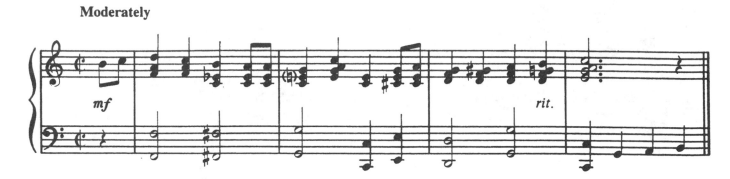

1. FROS - TY, THE SNOW MAN was a jol - ly hap - py soul,___ With a
2. FROS - TY, THE SNOW MAN knew the sun was hot that day,___ So he

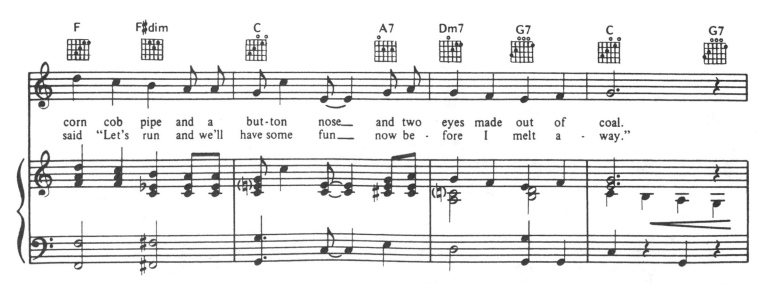

corn cob pipe and a but-ton nose___ and two eyes made out of coal.
said "Let's run and we'll have some fun___ now be - fore I melt a - way."

Frosty the Snowman - 3 - 1

76

Frosty the Snowman - 3 - 3

THE GIFT

Words and Music by
JIM BRICKMAN and
TOM DOUGLAS

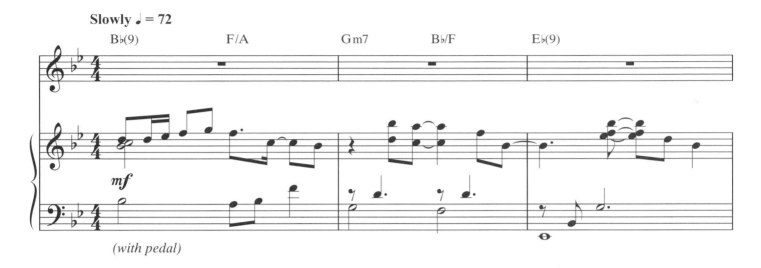

The Gift - 5 - 1

Chorus:

You're the an-swer when I prayed_ I would find some-one, and, ba-by, I___ found you._

___ And all I want___ is to hold___ you for-ev-er.___ And all I need_

___ is you more___ ev-'ry day.___ You saved my heart___ from be-ing

bro-ken a-part.___ You gave your love a-way, and I'm thank-ful ev-'ry day for the

Verse 2:

2. Watch-ing as you soft-ly__ sleep. What I'd give if I__ could__ keep just this mo-ment. If

on-ly time__ stood still. But the col-ors fade_____ a-way and the years will make us__ gray.__

__ But, ba-by, in my eyes,__ you'll still be beau-ti-ful.__ And all I want__

GO TELL IT ON THE MOUNTAIN

NEGRO SPIRITUAL

GOD IS WITH US

Words and Music by
WAYNE KIRKPATRICK

Chorus:

rain-ing down   on   the   world to-night; there's a   pres-ence here,   I   can___ tell.   God is

in___   us,   God   is   for___   us,   God   is   with us,   Em - man - u - el.   He's the

Sav - ior   we   have   been   pray-ing for,   in   our   hum - ble hearts   He   will___ dwell.   God is

in___   us,   God   is   for___   us,   God   is   with us,   Em - man - u - el.

GROWN-UP CHRISTMAS LIST

Words and Music by
DAVID FOSTER and
LINDA THOMPSON JENNER

Grown-Up Christmas List - 5 - 1

HALLELUJAH! CHORUS

(from *The Messiah*)

By GEORGE FRIDERIC HANDEL

Allegro moderato (♩ = 88)

Hal - le - lu - jah! Hal - le - lu - jah! Hal-le-lu - jah! Hal-le-lu - jah! Hal -

le - lu - jah! Hal - le - lu - jah! Hal - le - lu - jah! Hal-le -

Hallelujah! Chorus - 8 - 1

98

Lords. And He shall reign for-

ev - er and ev - er. King of Kings and Lord of

Lords. Hal - le - lu - jah! Hal - le - lu - jah! Hal - le - lu - jah! Hal - le -

Largo
ff

lu - jah! Hal - le - lu - jah!

ff

HARK! THE HERALD ANGELS SING

Words by
CHARLES WESLEY

Music by
FELIX MENDELSSOHN

HERE WE COME A-CAROLING
(The Wassail Song)

Old English

With spirit

Verse:

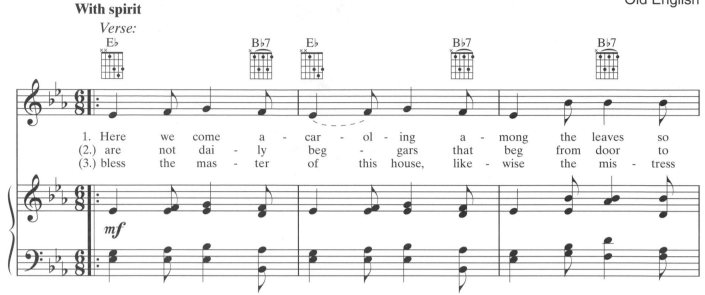

1. Here we come a-car-ol-ing a-mong the leaves so
(2.) are not dai-ly beg-gars that beg from door to
(3.) bless the mas-ter of this house, like-wise the mis-tress

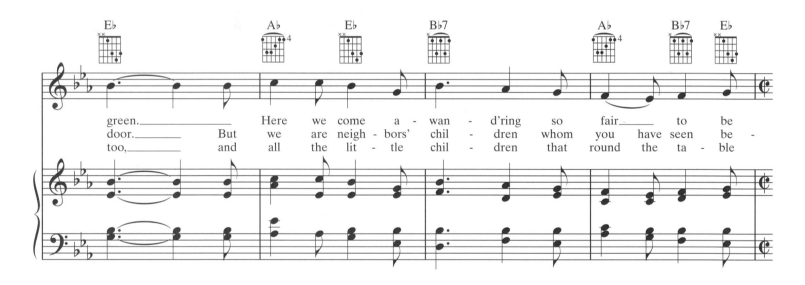

green._____ Here we come a-wan-d'ring so fair_____ to be
door._____ But we are neigh-bors' chil-dren whom you have seen be-
too,_____ and all the lit-tle chil-dren that round the ta-ble

Chorus:

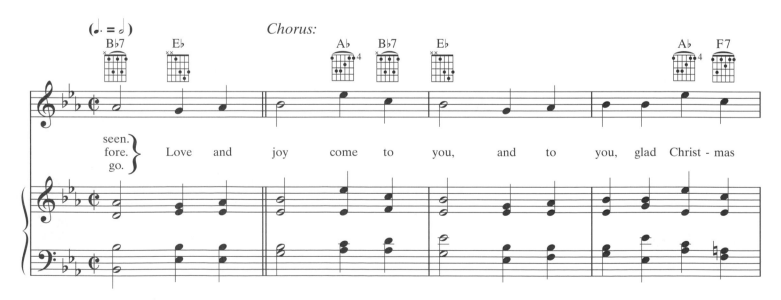

seen.
fore. Love and joy come to you, and to you, glad Christ-mas
go.

Here We Come A-Caroling - 2 - 1

HAVE YOURSELF A MERRY
LITTLE CHRISTMAS

Words and Music by
HUGH MARTIN and RALPH BLANE

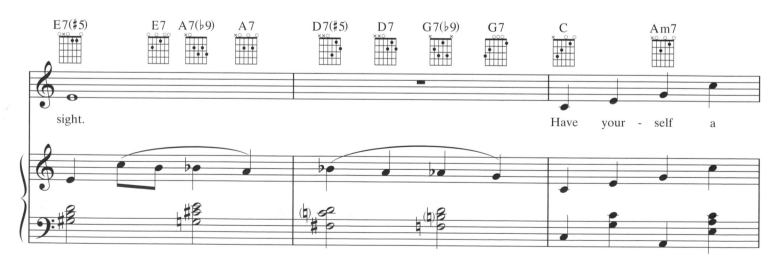

Have Yourself a Merry Little Christmas - 3 - 1

Have Yourself a Merry Little Christmas - 3 - 2

(There's No Place Like)
HOME FOR THE HOLIDAYS

Words by
AL STILLMAN

Music by
ROBERT ALLEN

Oh, there's no place like home for the hol-i-days,

'cause no mat-ter how far-a-way you roam,

{ when you pine for the sun-shine of a
{ if you want to be hap-py in a

I WANT AN OLD-FASHIONED CHRISTMAS

Words by
FLORENCE TARR

Music by
FAY FOSTER

I want an old-fash-ioned Christ-mas with

toys and gifts for all, with stock-ings hang-ing from the

fire-place, and a pine tree stand-ing tall. I

I Want an Old-Fashioned Christmas - 4 - 1

I'LL BE HOME FOR CHRISTMAS

Words by
KIM GANNON

Music by
WALTER KENT

I'll Be Home for Christmas - 3 - 1

IT'S THE MOST WONDERFUL TIME OF THE YEAR

Words and Music by
EDDIE POLA and GEORGE WYLE

It's the Most Wonderful Time of the Year - 3 - 1

122

JINGLE BELL ROCK

Words and Music by
JOE BEAL and JIM BOOTHE

Jin-gle-bell, Jin-gle-bell, Jin-gle-bell rock.___ Jin-gle-bell swing and jin-gle-bells ring. Snow-in' and blow-in' up bush-els of fun,

Jingle Bell Rock - 3 - 1

JINGLE BELLS

Words and Music by
JAMES PIERPONT

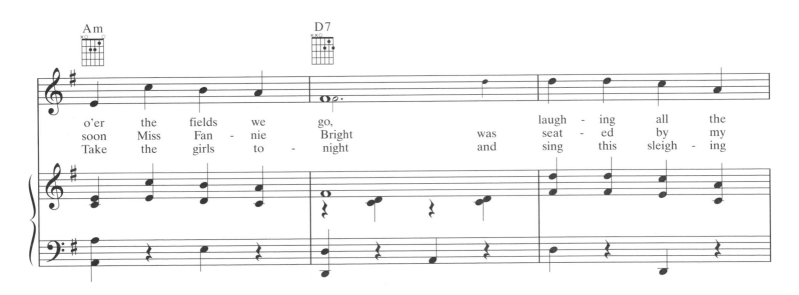

Jingle Bells - 3 - 1

JOY TO THE WORLD

Words by
ISAAC WATTS

Music by
GEORGE F. HANDEL

LAST CHRISTMAS

Words and Music by
GEORGE MICHAEL

Moderately steady beat ♩ = 108

Ah,_____ ooo, whoa,_____ ahh._____

Verse 1 (sing 1st time only):

1.Once bit-ten and twice shy,_____ I keep my dis-tance but

Verse 2 (sing 2nd time only):

2. A crowd-ed room, friends with tired__ eyes,___ I'm hid-ing from you

tears still catch__ my eye.___ Tell me, ba - by, do you rec-og-nize__ me?

and your soul__ of ice.___ My god, I thought you were some-one to re-ly__ on.

LET IT SNOW! LET IT SNOW! LET IT SNOW!

Words by
SAMMY CAHN

Music by
JULE STYNE

Oh, the weather outside is frightful, but the fire is so delightful, and since we've no place to go, let it snow, let it snow, let it snow! It

Let it Snow! Let it Snow! Let it Snow! - 3 - 1

LET THERE BE PEACE ON EARTH
(Let It Begin With Me)

Words and Music by
SY MILLER and JILL JACKSON

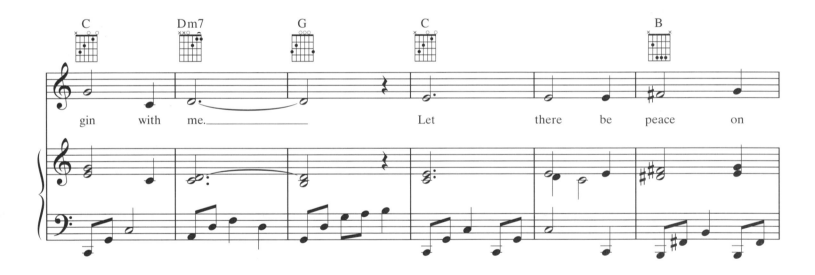

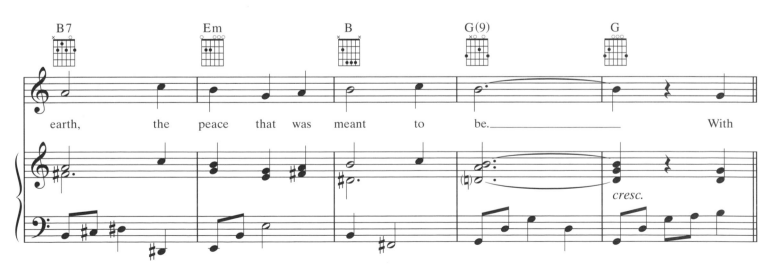

Let There Be Peace on Earth - 3 - 1

THE LITTLE DRUMMER BOY

Words and Music by
HARRY SIMEONE, HENRY ONORATI
and KATHERINE DAVIS

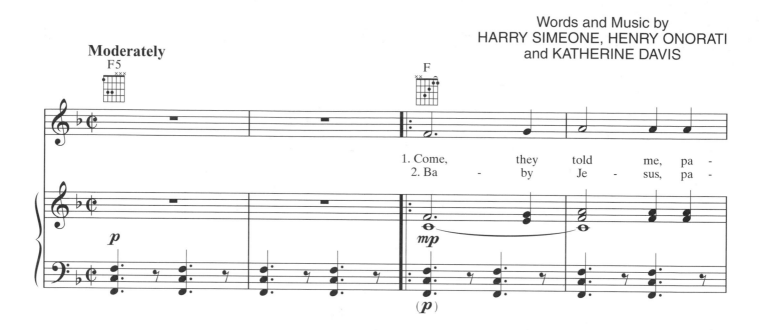

The Little Drummer Boy - 4 - 1

on___ my drum?___

3. Mar - y nod - ded, pa - rum pum pum pum,___

the ox and lamb kept time, pa - rum pum pum pum.___

I played my drum for Him, pa - rum pum pum pum,___

I played my best for Him, pa - rum pum pum pum, rum pum pum pum,

rum pum pum pum.

Slower

Then He smiled at me, pa - rum pum pum pum,

me and my drum.

The Little Drummer Boy - 4 - 4

THE LITTLE DRUMMER BOY/PEACE ON EARTH

PEACE ON EARTH:
Words by
ALAN KOHAN
Music by
LARRY GROSSMAN
and IAN FRASER

THE LITTLE DRUMMER BOY:
Words and Music by
HARRY SIMEONE, HENRY ONORATI
and KATHERINE DAVIS

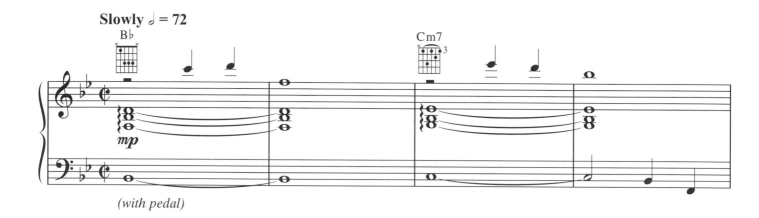

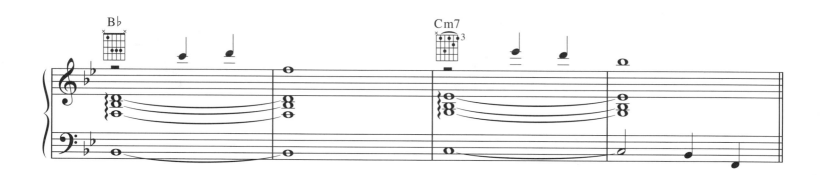

The Little Drummer Boy/Peace on Earth - 5 - 1

The Little Drummer Boy/Peace on Earth - 5 - 4

152

THESE ARE THE SPECIAL TIMES

Words and Music by
DIANE WARREN

Verse:

1. In these mo - ments, mo - ments of our lives, all the
2. With each mo - ment, mo - ment pass - ing by, we'll make

world is____ ours,____ and this world is so right.____
mem - o - ries____ that will last all our lives.____
as

These Are the Special Times - 5 - 1

THE MARVELOUS TOY

Words and Music by
TOM PAXTON

Moderately

1. When

Verse:

I was just a wee lit-tle lad, full of health and joy, my

2.3.4. *See additional lyrics*

fa-ther home-ward came one night and gave to me a toy. A

won-der to be-hold it was, with man-y col-ors bright, and the

The Marvelous Toy - 2 - 1

Verse 2:
The first time that I picked it up, I had a big surprise,
For right on its bottom were two big buttons that looked like big green eyes.
I first pushed one and then the other, and then I twisted its lid,
And when I set it down again, here is what it did:
(To Chorus 2:)

Verse 3:
It first marched left and then marched right and then marched under a chair,
And when I looked where it had gone, it wasn't even there!
I started to sob and my daddy laughed, for he knew that I would find
When I turned around my marvelous toy, chugging from behind.
(To Chorus 3:)

Verse 4:
Well, the years have gone by too quickly, it seems, and I have my own little boy.
And yesterday I gave him my marvelous little toy.
His eyes nearly popped right out of his head, and he gave a squeal of glee.
Neither one of us knows just what it is, but he loves it, just like me.
(To Chorus 4:)

Chorus 4:
It still goes "zip" when it moves, and "bop" when it stops,
And "whirr" when it stands still.
I never knew just what it was
And I guess I never will.

The Marvelous Toy - 2 - 2

MARY, DID YOU KNOW?

Words and Music by
MARK LOWRY and
BUDDY GREENE

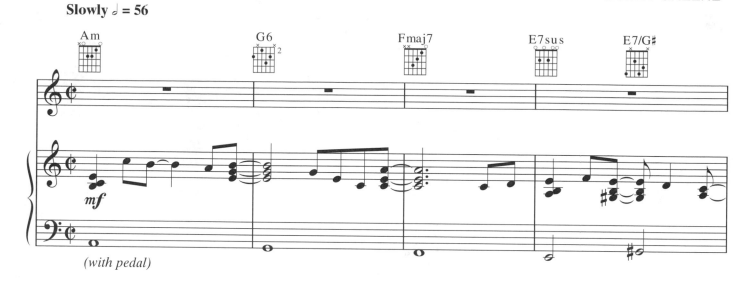

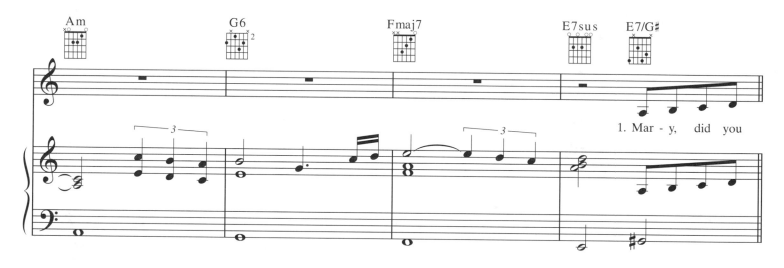

Mary, Did You Know? - 4 - 1

NATIVITY CAROL

Words and Music by
JOHN RUTTER

Andante tranquillo ♩ = 108

1. Born in a sta - ble so bare, Born so long a go. Born 'neath light of star
2. Cra - dled by moth - er so fair, Ten - der her lul - la - by. O - ver her Son so dear
3. Wise men from dis - tant far land, Shep - herds from star - ry hills Wor - ship this babe so rare,
4. Love in that sta - ble was born In - to our hearts to flow. In - no - cent dream - ing babe,

He who loved us so.
An - gel hosts fill the sky.
Hearts with His warmth He fills.
Make me thy love to know.

Nativity Carol - 2 - 2

O CHRISTMAS TREE
(O Tannenbaum)

TRADITIONAL

Moderately

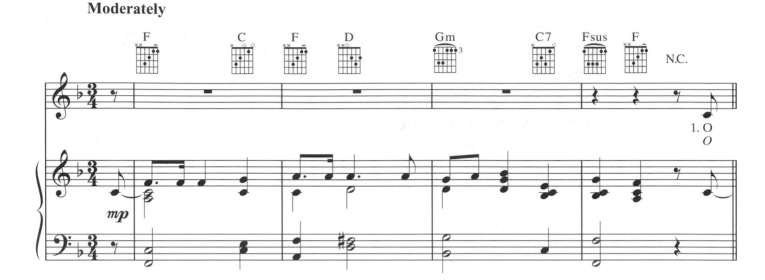

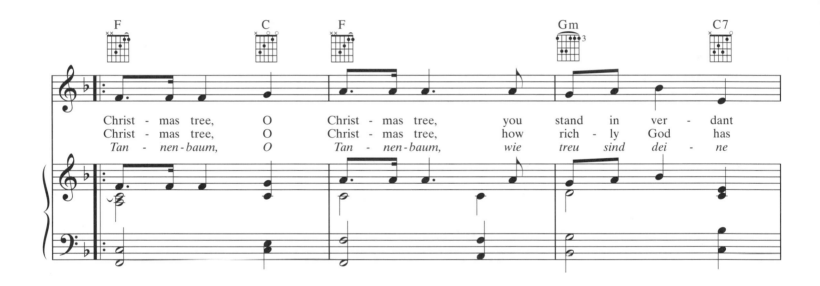

Christ - mas tree, O Christ - mas tree, you stand in ver - dant
Christ - mas tree, O Christ - mas tree, how rich - ly God has
Tan - nen - baum, O Tan - nen - baum, wie treu sind dei - ne

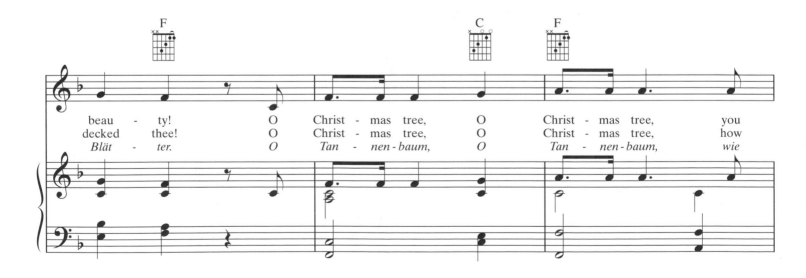

beau - ty! O Christ - mas tree, O Christ - mas tree, you
decked thee! O Christ - mas tree, O Christ - mas tree, how
Blät - ter. O Tan - nen - baum, O Tan - nen - baum, wie

O Christmas Tree - 2 - 1

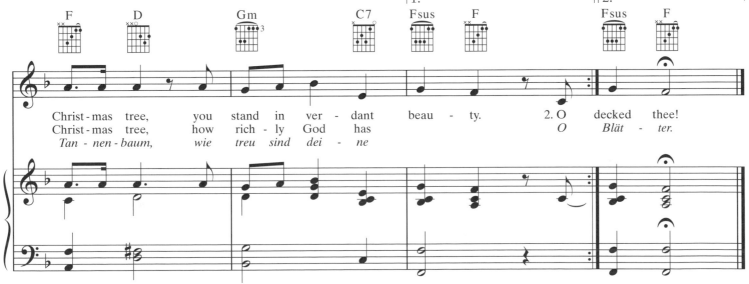

O HOLY NIGHT
(Cantique de Noël)

Words and Music by
J. S. DWIGHT and ADOLPHE ADAM

Majestically

1. O   ho - ly
2. Led   by the
3. Tru - ly He

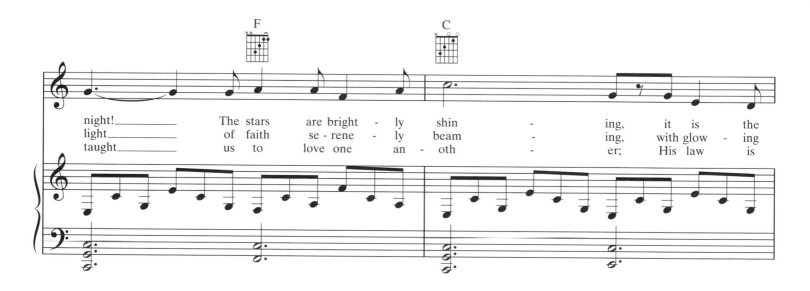

night!_____ The stars   are bright - ly shin   - ing, it is   the
light_____ of faith   se - rene - ly beam   - ing, with glow - ing
taught_____ us to   love one   an - oth   - er; His law   is

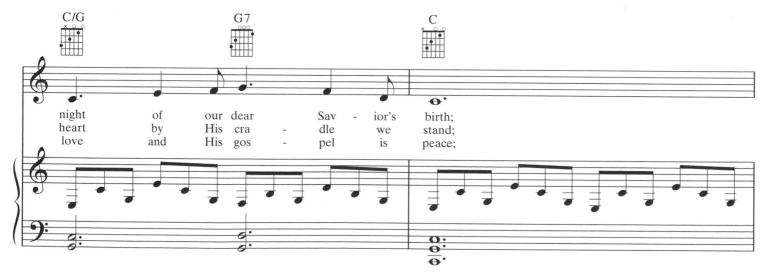

night   of   our dear   Sav - ior's   birth;
heart   by   His cra - dle   we   stand;
love   and His gos - pel   is   peace;

O Holy Night - 4 - 1

long lay the world_____ in sin and sor - row
so led by light_____ of a star sweet - ly
Chains shall He break, for the slave is our

pin - - ing, till He ap - peared and the soul felt its
gleam - - ing, here came the wise and men from the O - rient
broth - - er, and in His name all op - pres - sion shall

worth. A thrill of hope, the
land. The King of kings lay
cease. With hymns of joy in

wea - ry world re - joic - es, for yon - der breaks a
thus in low - ly man - ger, in all our tri - als
grate - ful cho - rus rais - ing, let ev - 'ry heart a -

O Holy Night - 4 - 2

O Holy Night - 4 - 4

O LITTLE TOWN OF BETHLEHEM

Words by
PHILLIPS BROOKS

Music by
LEWIS H. REDNER

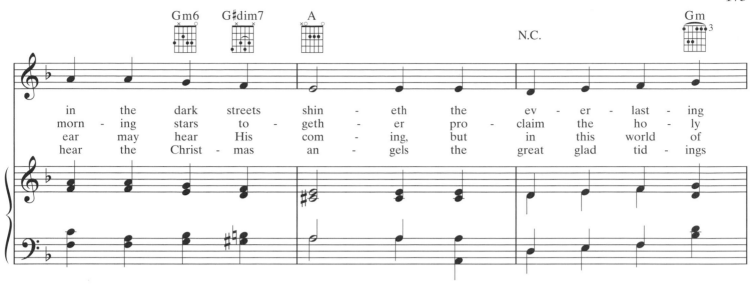

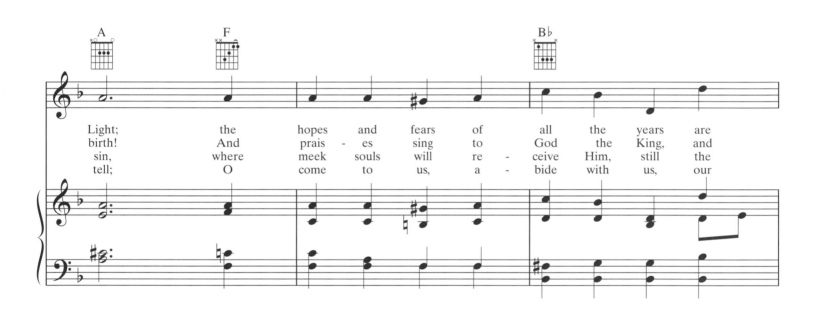

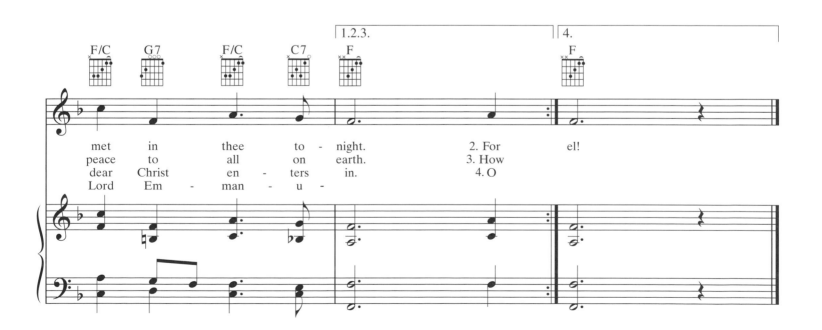

THE PRAYER

Italian Lyric by
ALBERTO TESTA and TONY RENIS

Words and Music by
CAROLE BAYER SAGER and DAVID FOSTER

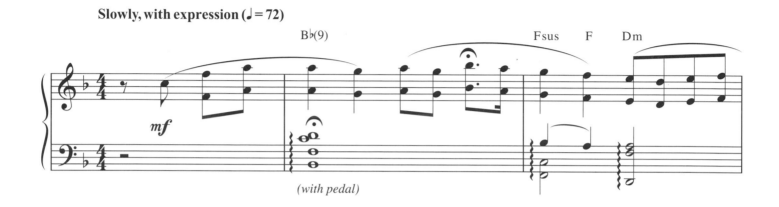

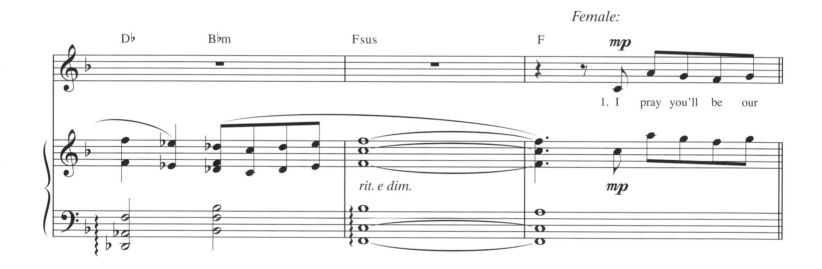

Verse 2:

Verse 3:

Chorus:

SANTA BABY

Words and Music by
JOAN JAVITS, PHILIP SPRINGER
and TONY SPRINGER

SANTA CLAUS IS COMIN' TO TOWN

Words by
HAVEN GILLESPIE

Music by
J. FRED COOTS

Santa Claus Is Comin' to Town - 5 - 1

188

SILENT NIGHT

Words and Music by
JOSEPH MOHR and
FRANZ GRUBER

SLEIGH RIDE

Words by
MITCHELL PARISH

Music by
LEROY ANDERSON

THE TWELVE DAYS OF CHRISTMAS

TRADITIONAL ENGLISH

The Twelve Days of Christmas - 8 - 4

Verse 10:

par - tridge_ in a pear tree. 10. On the tenth day of Christ-mas, my true love sent to me

tens lords a - leap-ing, nine la - dies danc-ing, eight maids a - milk-ing, sev - en swans a - swim-ming,

six geese a - lay-ing, five gold - en rings, four___ call - ing birds,

three French hens, two___ tur - tle doves, and a par - tridge in a pear tree. 11. On the e -

WE WISH YOU A MERRY CHRISTMAS

TRADITIONAL ENGLISH FOLK SONG

From THE POLAR EXPRESS

WHEN CHRISTMAS COMES TO TOWN

Lyrics by
GLEN BALLARD

Music by
ALAN SILVESTRI

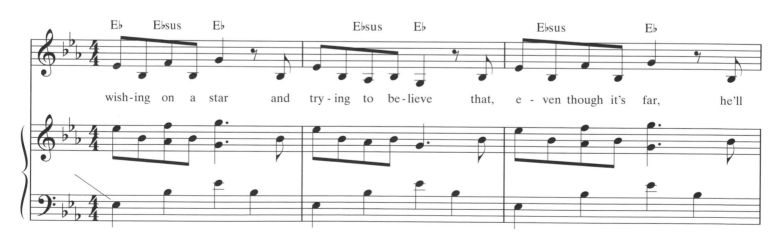

When Christmas Comes to Town - 6 - 1

That's all I want when Christ-mas comes_____ to

town.

WEXFORD CAROL

Traditional,
Arranged by DAVID DOWNES

Very slowly, rubato throughout ♩ = 60

Wexford Carol - 5 - 1

Wexford Carol - 5 - 4

did our Sav - ior Christ be-hold. With-in a man - ger He was laid,___ and___

mp Ooo.___ *p* Ooo.___

by___ His side___ the vir-gin maid, as long fore-told up -

Ooo.___ As long fore-told___ up - *mp*

on that morn there was a bless-ed___ Mes - si - ah born.

on that morn.___ Ooo.___ *pp*

WINTER WONDERLAND

Words by
DICK SMITH

Music by
FELIX BERNARD

Refrain:

geth - er!_____ Sleigh - bells ring, are you lis - t'nin'? In the lane, snow is glis - t'nin'. A beau - ti - ful sight,__ we're hap - py to - night,__ walk - in' in a win - ter won - der - land! Gone a - way is the blue - bird, here to

YOU'RE A MEAN ONE, MR. GRINCH

(from *How the Grinch Stole Christmas*)

Lyrics by
DR. SEUSS

Music by
ALBERT HAGUE

You're a Mean One, Mr. Grinch - 2 - 1

Verse 2:
You're a monster, Mr. Grinch!
Your heart's an empty hole.
Your brain is full of spiders,
You've got garlic in your soul, Mr. Grinch!
I wouldn't touch you with a
Thirty-nine-and-one-half-foot pole.

Verse 3:
You're a foul one, Mr. Grinch!
You're a nasty-wasty skunk!
Your heart is full of unwashed socks,
Your soul is full of gunk, Mr. Grinch!
The three words that best describe you
Are as follows and I quote:
Stink! - Stank! - Stunk!

Verse 4:
You're a vile one, Mr. Grinch!
You have termites in your smile.
You have all the tender sweetness
Of a seasick crocodile, Mr. Grinch!
(Spoken:) And given the choice between the two of you
I'd take the seasick crocodile.

Verse 5:
You're a rotter, Mr. Grinch!
You're the king of sinful sots.
Your heart's a dead tomato
Spotched with moldy, purple spots, Mr. Grinch...
(Spoken:) Your soul is an appalling dumpheap
overflowing with the most disgraceful assortment of
deplorable rubbish imaginable, mangled up in
...Tangled-up knots.

Verse 6:
You nauseate me, Mr. Grinch!
With a nauseous, super naus.
You're a crooked jerkey jockey
And you drive a crooked hoss, Mr. Grinch!
(Spoken:) You're a three-decker Sauerkraut
and toadstool sandwich
...with arsenic sauce.

You're a Mean One, Mr. Grinch - 2 - 2

WIZARDS IN WINTER

(Instrumental)

Music by
PAUL O'NEILL and ROBERT KINKEL

Moderately fast ♩ = 144

Wizards in Winter - 7 - 6